Discovery Kids

# CUTEST BABY ANIMALS OF ALL TIME

by Mari Bolte

PEBBLE
a capstone imprint

Published by Pebble, an imprint of Capstone
1710 Roe Crest Drive, North Mankato, Minnesota 56003
capstonepub.com



Library of Congress Cataloging-in-Publication Data is available on the Library of Congress website.

ISBN: 9798875256424 (hardcover)
ISBN: 9798875256370 (paperback)
ISBN: 9798875256387 (ebook PDF)

Summary: Baby animals make you say "aww!" Some are fluffy. Some are super small. Others are simply adorable. But which one is the C.O.A.T.—Cutest Of All Time? Each baby animal is scored in three cute categories, allowing readers to compare the totals of 16 babies to find out the winner.

**Editorial Credits**
Editor: Erika L. Shores; Designer: Dina Her; Media Researcher: Rebekah Hubstenberger; Production Specialist: Tori Abraham

**Image Credits**
Dreamstime: © Tarpan, 6; Getty Images: Bruce Shafer/Stocktrek Images, 12, Fuse, 19 (penguin), iStock/CraigRJD, back cover (left), 7 (kangaroo), iStock/Farinosa, 8 (bear), iStock/GlobalP, front cover (bottom middle), John James, 16 (giraffe), Martin Ruegner, back cover (right), 3 (right), 21 (penguin), 22, Winfried Wisniewski, 11; Shutterstock: bluedog studio, front cover (bottom right), 15, Eric Isselee (panda), 1, 14, Holly Kuchera, 13, Johan Buchner, front cover (bottom left), KYRYCHENKO ANASTASIIA, 7 (doodle glasses), lesyau_art (stars and winner ribbon), throughout, Look_Studio, 9 (doodle stars), Mark F Lotterhand, 18, Masharii (doodle bib), front cover, 16, Nadiinko (stars), front and back cover, 1, Passakorn Umpornmaha, 5, Petr Bonek, 3 (giraffe), Polina Tomtosova (doodle hearts, flowers, shooting star, emphasis lines), throughout, Rebellion Works (doodle baby accessories, stars), cover and throughout, Rosa Jay (fennec fox), 1, 10, Voin_Sveta, 21 (doodle crown), wasapohn (doodle hat), 1, 10, wildestanimal, 9 (whale), WilleeCole Photography, 17, Wirestock Creators, 4, yuliia_studzinska, front cover (doodle headband), Zaie (dot background), cover and throughout

Printed and bound in China. 006460

# CUTES FACE OFF

Baby animals are cute. But which baby animal is the Cutest Of All Time (C.O.A.T.)?

We paired up 16 wild babies in a who's cuter challenge. Each animal is given one to five stars in three categories. Check out each animal's total cute factor. At the end, a chart helps you discover who is the C.O.A.T.!

## ELEPHANT

Elephant calves learn to use their **trunks** by touching. Poke, poke! Very young calves suck on their trunks. It's just like a baby human sucking their thumb.

**Cutest Thing About Me:**
Flappy ears!

**Fluffiness:** ★☆☆☆☆

**Aww Factor:** ★★★★★

**Playfulness:** ★★★★★

**Total Cute Factor:** 11

**Cutest Thing About Me:**
Totally kissable snout!

| | |
|---|---|
| **Fluffiness:** | ★☆☆☆☆ |
| **Aww Factor:** | ★★★★★ |
| **Playfulness:** | ★★★☆☆ |

**Total Cute Factor: 9**

## PYGMY HIPPO

**Pygmy** hippo babies are totally adorable. A calf's big "yawn" means back off! Then it throws water with its mouth. Watch out! You're in the splash zone!

## WEDDELL SEAL

Weddell seals live in Antarctica. Brr! Seal pups have fuzzy, fluffy fur. The pups stay warm playing in cold ocean water.

## RED KANGAROO

Baby kangaroos are called joeys. At birth, joeys are the size of a jellybean. They stay in their mom's pouch for nearly 200 days. When they are grown, they hop, hop, hop everywhere.

**Cutest Thing About Me:**
White chest!

**Fluffiness:** ★☆☆☆☆

**Aww Factor:** ★★★☆☆

**Playfulness:** ★★★☆☆

**Total Cute Factor: 7**

## BROWN BEAR

Brown bear cubs are born in winter. They snuggle up to their moms until spring. Then, they learn to find food. Big paws and sharp claws help them dig for treats.

**Cutest Thing About Me:**
Little round ears!

| | |
|---|---|
| **Fluffiness:** | ★★★★☆ |
| **Aww Factor:** | ★★★★☆ |
| **Playfulness:** | ★★☆☆☆ |

**Total Cute Factor: 10**

## HUMPBACK WHALE

Big baby! Humpback whale calves weigh as much as six refrigerators. They grow fast drinking rich milk from their mothers. The milk is thick like toothpaste!

**Cutest Thing About Me:**
Flappy flippers!

Fluffiness: ☆☆☆☆☆

Aww Factor: ★★★☆☆

Playfulness: ★★★☆☆

Total Cute Factor: 6

**Cutest Thing About Me:**
Huge, wiggly ears!

**Fluffiness:** ★★★☆☆

**Aww Factor:** ★★★★★

**Playfulness:** ★★★★☆

**Total Cute Factor: 12**

## FENNEC FOX

Some people call them kits. Others call them pups. No matter what fennec fox babies are called, they're cute. Fennec foxes are the tiniest foxes. They are smaller than a pet cat.

## SNOWY OWL

Snowy owlets are covered with fuzzy feathers called down. They leave the nest after three weeks. They can't fly yet. Instead, they waddle around after their moms and dads. Wait up! I have little wings!

**Cutest Thing About Me:**
So soft and fluffy!

**Fluffiness:** ★★★★★
**Aww Factor:** ★★★★★
**Playfulness:** ★☆☆☆☆

**Total Cute Factor: 11**

**Cutest Thing About Me:**
Look at that smile!

**Fluffiness:** ☆☆☆☆☆
**Aww Factor:** ★★★★★
**Playfulness:** ☆☆☆☆☆

**Total Cute Factor: 5**

## PUFFERFISH

Don't scare me, I'll puff! Baby pufferfish can't swim fast. They puff up when something scary swims by. Some pufferfish are spiky. Others are smooth. And they are all full of poison. No cuddling allowed!

## BEAVER

Beaver kits can swim hours after being born. Their **webbed** feet and wide, flat tails help them get around in the water. With their front paws, beavers grab sticks and snacks.

**Cutest Thing About Me:**
Boopable snoot!

**Fluffiness:** ★☆☆☆☆
**Aww Factor:** ★★★★☆
**Playfulness:** ★★☆☆☆

**Total Cute Factor: 7**

# GIANT PANDA

Their moms may be big, but panda cubs are born small. Newborns are about as long as a stick of butter. Baby pandas grow fast. They eat 14 times a day. That's a lot of snacks!

**Cutest Thing About Me:**
Adorable black eyes and ears!

**Fluffiness:** ★★★☆☆

**Aww Factor:** ★★★★★

**Playfulness:** ★★★★★

**Total Cute Factor: 13**

Cutest Thing About Me:
Long, striped tail!

Fluffiness: ★★★☆☆

Aww Factor: ★★★★☆

Playfulness: ★★★★★

Total Cute Factor: 12

## PYGMY MARMOSET

Pygmy marmosets are the smallest **primates** on Earth. Newborns are about the size of a human thumb. Even when they are grown up, they are not big. Hold out your hands. An adult pygmy marmoset could fit in them.

## GIRAFFE

Giraffe calves come crashing into the world. These babies fall 5 to 6 feet (1.5 to 1.8 meters) when they are born. The fall helps them wake up. After an hour, calves are up and running around. Whee!

**Cutest Thing About Me:**
Smiling lips!

**Fluffiness:** ★☆☆☆☆

**Aww Factor:** ★★★★★

**Playfulness:** ★★☆☆☆

**Total Cute Factor: 8**

## WHITETAIL DEER

Fawns stay safe in tall grass while their mothers eat lunch. But when lunch is over, it's time to play. They leap and run as fast as they can. They chase their deer friends in circles. Boing, boing!

**Cutest Thing About Me:**
Twitchy tail!

**Fluffiness:** ★☆☆☆☆
**Aww Factor:** ★★★★★
**Playfulness:** ★★★☆☆

**Total Cute Factor: 9**

**Cutest Thing About Me:**
A nose for digging in the dirt!

Fluffiness: ☆☆☆☆☆
Aww Factor: ★★★★★
Playfulness: ★★★★☆

**Total Cute Factor: 9**

## HOGNOSE SNAKE

Newborn hognose snakes are called snakelets. They look like mini adults. They are tiny, but they try to act big. When they get scared, they make their faces puffy to look tough. Sometimes they flip over and play dead.

## EMPEROR PENGUIN

Life on the ice is chilly. To stay warm, emperor penguin chicks have downy feathers. When it gets really cold, they snuggle up in their mom or dad's **brood pouch.**

**Cutest Thing About Me:**
Teeny tiny beak!

| | |
|---|---|
| Fluffiness: | ★★★★★ |
| Aww Factor: | ★★★★☆ |
| Playfulness: | ★★★★★ |

**Total Cute Factor: 14**

# CUTE FACTOR FACE OFF

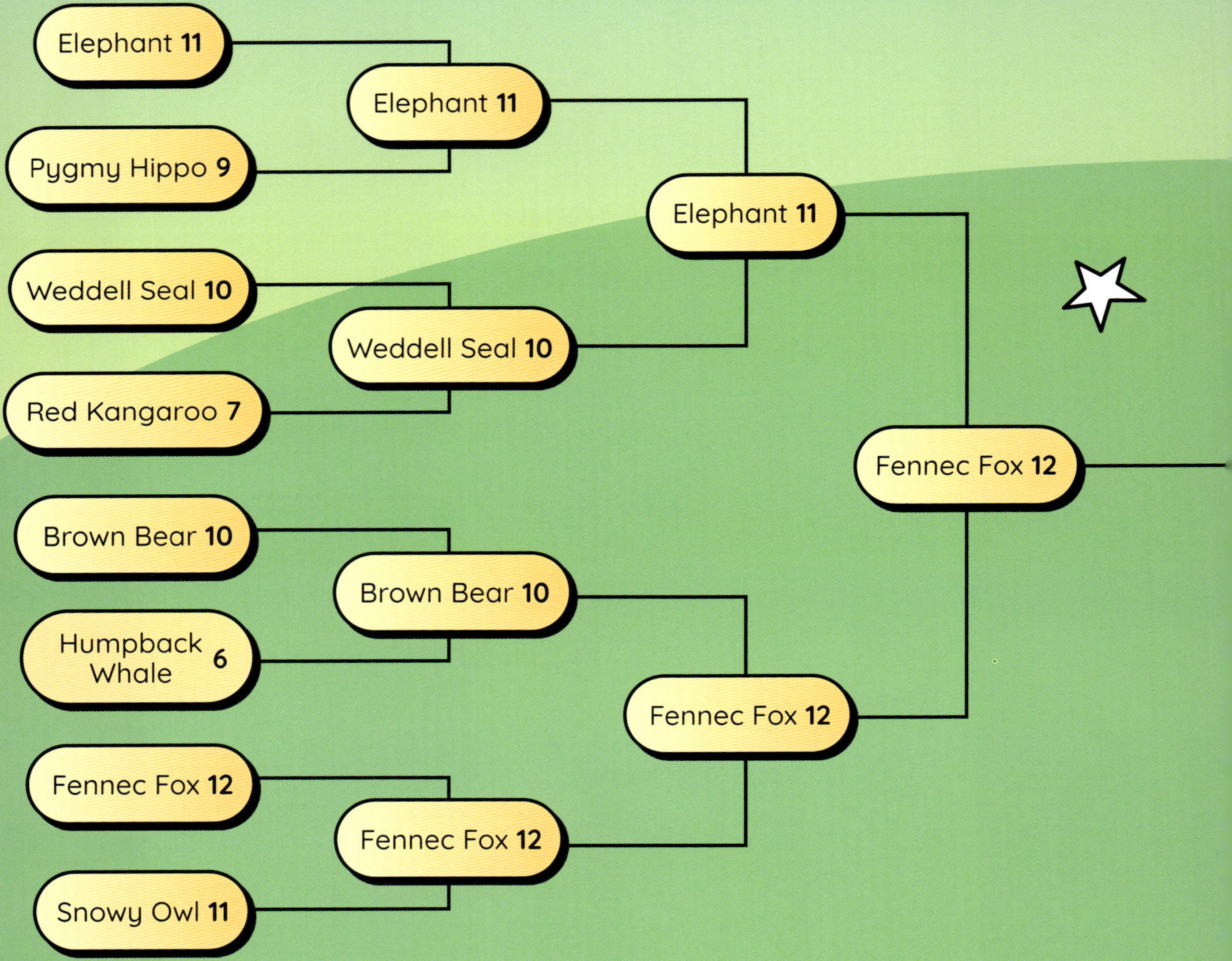

| Round 1 | Quarterfinal | Semifinal | Final |
|---|---|---|---|
| Elephant **11** vs. Pygmy Hippo **9** | Elephant **11** | | |
| Weddell Seal **10** vs. Red Kangaroo **7** | Weddell Seal **10** | Elephant **11** | |
| Brown Bear **10** vs. Humpback Whale **6** | Brown Bear **10** | | |
| Fennec Fox **12** vs. Snowy Owl **11** | Fennec Fox **12** | Fennec Fox **12** | Fennec Fox **12** |

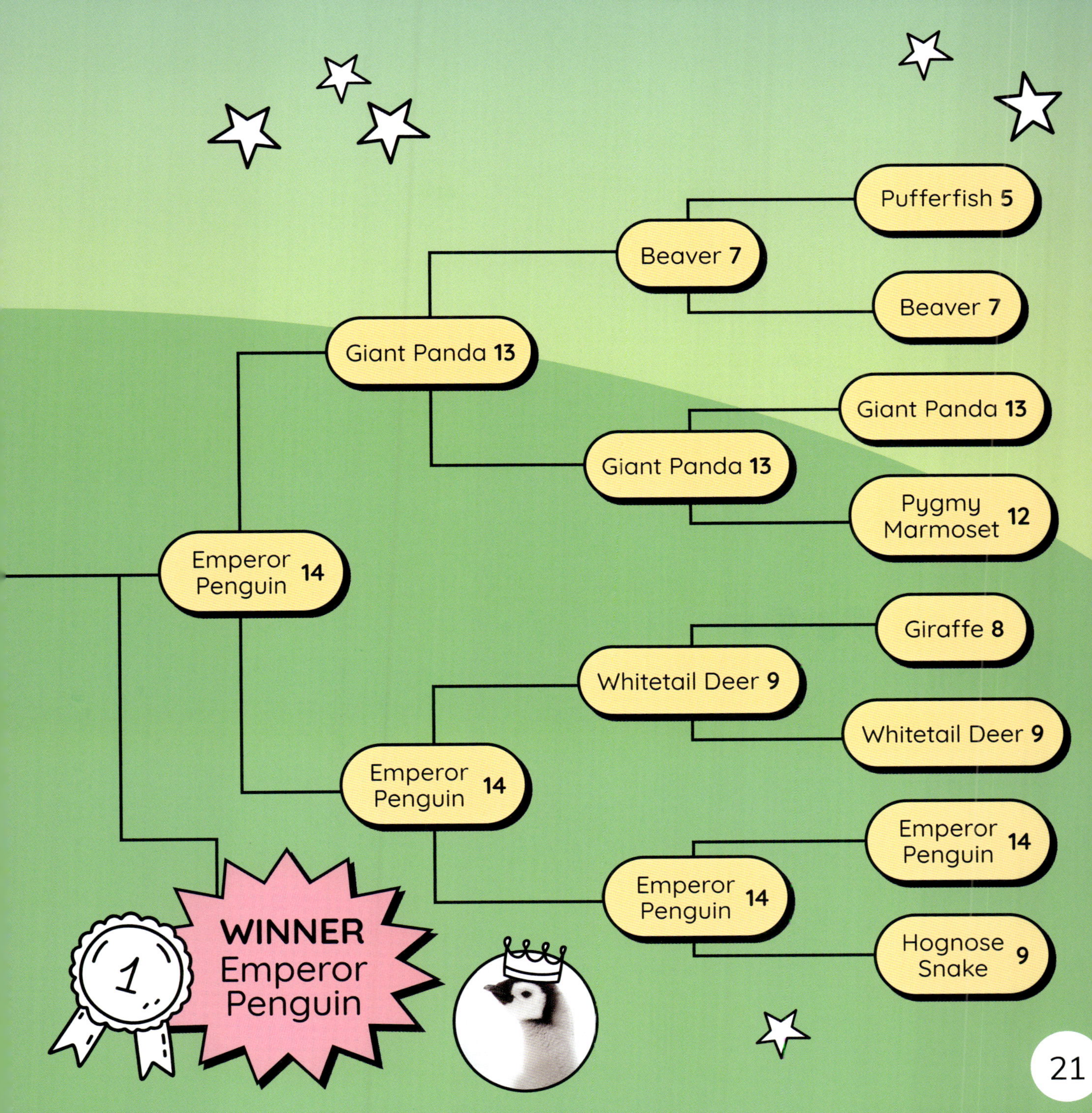
Pufferfish 5
Beaver 7
Beaver 7
Giant Panda 13
Giant Panda 13
Giant Panda 13
Pygmy Marmoset 12
Emperor Penguin 14
Giraffe 8
Whitetail Deer 9
Whitetail Deer 9
Emperor Penguin 14
Emperor Penguin 14
Emperor Penguin 14
Hognose Snake 9
WINNER
Emperor Penguin
1

# THE C.O.A.T.

It's fluffy. It's cuddly. It's adorably "aww"-some. Its total cute factor makes it our winner. Emperor penguin chicks are the Cutest Of All Time!

Do you agree? Go back and give each animal your own score. Make a new chart on a separate piece of paper. Maybe a different animal will be your winner.

# GLOSSARY

**brood pouch** (BROOD POWCH)—a flap of skin that keeps eggs or baby animals warm

**primate** (PRYE-mate)—any member of the group of intelligent animals that includes humans, apes, and monkeys

**pygmy** (PIG-mee)—an animal much smaller than more typical kinds

**trunk** (TRUNK)—an elephant's long nose and upper lip

**webbed** (WEBD)—feet with wide flaps of skin between the toes

# INDEX



# ABOUT THE AUTHOR

Mari Bolte is the author and editor of hundreds of children's books. Every book is her favorite book as long as the readers learned something and enjoyed themselves!